© Heinemann Educational Books Ltd 1991

First published in 1991 by
Heinemann Children's Reference
a division of Heinemann Educational Books Ltd
Halley Court, Jordan Hill, Oxford OX2 8EJ

OXFORD LONDON EDINBURGH
MADRID PARIS ATHENS BOLOGNA
MELBOURNE SYDNEY AUCKLAND SINGAPORE
TOKYO IBADAN NAIROBI GABORONE
HARARE PORTSMOUTH NH(USA)

ISBN 0 431 00339 4

British Library Cataloguing in Publication Data
Bailey, Donna
    We live in Spain
    1.   Spain. Social life
    I.   Title II.   Series
    946.083

Editorial consultant: Donna Bailey
Designed by Richard Garratt Design
Picture research by Jennifer Garratt

Photographs:
Cover: Spectrum Colour Library
Robert Harding Picture Library: title page, 5, 8, 14
Hutchison: 3 (J Pate), 6, 11 (Patricio Goycoolea), 13, 15, 16 (Nancy
    Durrell McKenna)
Spectrum Colour Library: 2, 4, 7, 10, 12, 17, 18, 20, 25, 26, 27, 28, 30, 31,
    32
Zefa: 9, 19, 21, 22, 23, 24, 29

Printed in Hong Kong

91 92 93 94 95 10 9 8 7 6 5 4 3 2 1

We Live in Spain

Donna Bailey

HEINEMANN

Hello! My name is Adela and
this is my little brother Juan.
We live in Seville, in southern Spain.
We are wearing our best clothes
because today is a special holiday.

Seville is a big city with
lots of parks and important buildings.
Hundreds of years ago the Moors of
North Africa came to Spain.
They built many fine buildings
in Seville.

Many of the houses today are built
in the Moorish style.
The houses are decorated with arches
and mosaics in different patterns
around the doorways and windows.

Our house is in a small courtyard
just off one of the side streets.
The trees in the courtyard help
keep the house cool in the summer
when the weather gets very hot.

After school we often go to
the Maria Luisa Park near our house.
Everybody likes to feed the white doves
in America Square.

In the evening you can usually
see a group of men playing bowls in
the park after work.

Sometimes we hire a rowing boat and
row round the Plaza de España
which is also in Maria Luisa Park.

Everyone in Seville knows the high tower
which is part of the Cathedral of Seville.
The Cathedral is the largest in Spain.
The famous explorer Christopher Columbus
is buried here.

Tourists often take a ride around
the city in a horse-drawn carriage.
The carriages wait for them just
outside the Cathedral.

The tourists usually visit the Golden Tower
on the river bank.
The Golden Tower was once part of
an old wall which guarded the port
of Seville.

Boats can still come up the river to
the port of Seville.
Fishermen cast their nets in
the early morning to catch fish
in the river.

When we go to visit my cousins who
live in the country we usually
have lunch on the way.
In the summer we sit outside to eat
because it is too hot indoors.

My uncle has sheep on his farm in the country not far from Seville. He also keeps some goats as well.

My cousin has a pet goat.
It is only a baby but it has
lost its mother.
My cousin looks after it and
feeds it with milk.

My aunt makes cheese from the goats' milk.
She presses the cheese into round baskets.
Later she will take the cheese to sell
in the market in Seville.

My favourite time in Seville is
during the April Fair.
Suddenly a city of tents appears on
the fairground just outside the city.
The tents are in rows with little streets
in between them.

During the three days of Seville's
April Fair the girls all dress up in
their special dresses.
They wear scarves round their necks and
flowers in their hair.

The men and horses all look their best too.
Some horses have embroidered saddles
and decorated bridles.

Most men wear short black jackets and stiff-brimmed grey or black Cordoban hats. Many men also wear decorated leather leggings over their trousers.

The women balance carefully behind
their partners, holding on with
one arm around the men's waists.
Other women ride their own horses.
They wear a similar costume to the men's.

The horses and riders parade up and down
the streets past the little canvas booths
called casetas.
Each caseta belongs to a group of
friends or a business.

The streets of the fairground are decorated with lights, flags and flowers.
Cars are not allowed but the streets are full of open carriages passing up and down.

Sometimes a whole family crams themselves
into a carriage for a ride around
the fairground.

Of course the mules pulling the carriage
have been decorated with flowers and
garlands as well.

Other families prefer to ride together
on one horse.
Perhaps they are going to the funfair.

26

There are lots of different things
to do at the funfair.
Riding a horse on the merry-go-round
is not so difficult if you have been
riding a real horse.

These children prefer the thrills and
bumps of a ride in a dodgem car.

The older girls wander up and down
the sidewalks past the casetas.
They stop to chat with their friends
about what they will do in the evening.

Suddenly there is a sound of hands
clapping out a catchy rhythm.
Two girls begin dancing a flamenco.
They stamp their feet to the rhythm.

Later on inside each caseta, the girls
will dance the flamenco until late
into the night.
They click their fingers and castanets
to the rhythm of the music.

The singing and dancing go on
until late in the night.
Nobody thinks of going to bed before
four o'clock in the morning!
Even the youngest children are allowed
to stay up late during the April Fair.

Index